GOOD SCIENCE

Ken Edwards

GOOD SCIENCE

POEMS 1983–1991

Some of these poems, in different versions, have appeared in:
Angels of Fire (Chatto & Windus, 1986), and in the magazines *Central Park*, *Critical Quarterly*, *Gargara*, *Horizontal Volcano*, *Ninth Decade*, *Oasis*, *RWC*, *Solicited Material*.
A sound version of "Lexical Dub" appeared as an audiocassette on Balsam Flex, *Lexical Dub, for Sarah Tisdall*, 1984.

Cover: Shoeing Horses I, from *L'Encyclopedie* of Denis Diderot.
Cover by Deborah Thomas.

ISBN: 0-937804-48-7
Library of Congress Catalog Card No. : 92-061309

This book was made possible, in part, by a grant from the New York State Council on the Arts.

Roof Books
are published by
Segue Foundation
303 East 8th Street
New York, New York 10009

CONTENTS

Preface:

A note to the reader on some self-imposed procedures in the making of this book, their use, and an indication of some possible responses

SEE CLEARLY with clear eyes. Be strong, harmonic and geological. Shun high-tech special effects. As a constant reminder of the possibilities, hold up a kaleidoscope to "our expanding universe". Do not always trust machines. Demonstrate a dispersal pattern reminiscent of, or at least seeming to be a synthesis. In the service of compassion, reduce all human aspirations to the brute matter of existence. Look at the world unflinchingly in the grey morning light. "Create a system, or be enslaved by another's." Relevant systems appear simultaneously as unsolved mystery and as ample evidence. Demonstrate relevance. Relevant systems have no content (specific) but plenty of formal designations (variable). Demonstrate variation. They spread, and cause the perspective to tilt; but they have no intent. Demonstrate intent. Where there is no intent, there is no dance, where there is no dance, there is no exactness, where there is no exactness, there is no death. Open the telephone book at random, call the number, when the person answers give the person the news, and hang up. Do not attempt explanation. Do not apologise.

Contort; invest a song. Practise "the fruity O, the piquant short i"; use "occasionally sarcastic typography". Call it the language. Hint at a place beyond language. Alternately speak, and indicate the silence beyond speech. Alternately add meaning to events, and take away their meaning. Do improvisation to pay the rent. Speak several languages; reject all language. Think in your mouth. Believe in verbal magic. Go on speech strike for six months. Remember "the code is not adequate to what needs to be said; it is not the language". Create something modern and intrinsic, sensitive and strong. Treat words with the contempt they deserve.

Learn everything you can, and forget everything you have learnt; do this on alternate days. Look at yourself straight in the face. Scorn the blandishments of songbirds. Laugh uncontrollably. Waste time. Groan. Throb. Consider whether "art is crime". Go to jail anyway. Stifle. Steam. Congest. Melt. Exinguish. Pour. Staunch. Curse. Sleep. Put the question squarely. Escape. Forget everything. Panic.

1

Take measures to illustrate your disquiet. Come to your senses. Don't be so stupid. Destroy the cadence of the line, the beauty of the image, the aptness of the metaphor. Cultivate a deliberately lush and sensuous vocabulary, and then prune it savagely. Better still, shun all metaphors. Cultivate misunderstanding. Be reasonable. Collect useful facts, and facts about facts. Make them into a structure that is completely useless. Collect useless facts, and make them into a useful structure. Make textures and structures in the tentative region of the untried. Make a bridge for scholars, then at a crucial moment blow up the bridge. Set fire to all manuscripts. Make "every sentence ... a critique of reason". Persist. Involve everybody. Implicate everybody. Ingest. Undermine homoeostasis in language with a sense of balance overtipped by the non-programmed, i.e. anything could happen. Remember sensation of form is sensation of flow.

Replace experience with language. Replace form with design. Open all windows. Lie on the carpet. Think carefully. Abolish the floor. Eat your words. Destroy information. Nuzzle cups, bathe archipelagos, suck gold, number gravel, lift silk, carry animals, manufacture grief, parse hallucinations, swallow embers, suspect hostages, supervise deserts, ridicule buildings, hurl bones, research hunger, simmer books, sniff electricity, crush parapets, imagine clothes.

Never discount the opacity of language. Never attempt to communicate. Never form a kind of shell or armour round the subject. Never make absolute sense. By no means shun exactness. Do not attempt to make sense of "our culture". Never write what you expect to have written. Do not concern yourself with lyric significance. "Use the telephone instead of writing the poem." Avoid floral-phallic imagery. Do not however forget pleasure in the erotic multiplicity of sense. Never compromise. Never close for lunch. Reject validation. Accept overdetermination.

Be marginal and heat-seeking. Be glittering, leggy, inevitable. Be agitational, molecular, powerful, disparate, innumerable, blank, necessary, accurate, conscious, communal, conservative. Encourage relentless hope. Hope for "a liberty of unimaginable opulence". Hope for "a purely linguistic world". Hope for "a kind of chemical solution". Hope for "a state in which speech is at the same time more primitive and more sophisticated than in ordinary usage". Hope for "the transformation of the vertical". Surprise yourself.

Astonish others. Uncover "a content that pushes against social taboos otherwise not only untransgressed but unknown". Hope for "a textual body recognised by the fact that it is always endless, without ending". Take scientific notes. "Gulp down the tawny herds." Hope for "an explosion of verbal glass". Differentiate. Invent the language everybody already speaks. Make a contract with language; then break the contract. Imitate everybody; originate nothing. Tell lies rather than tell half-truths. Live without memory. Surround yourself with resources, and wait. Get rid of all resources, and act now.

Thanks to: Guillaume Apollinaire, William Blake, Lyn Hejinian, Hélène Cixous, Paul Goodman, John Vernon, Frank O'Hara, Jeff Nuttall, Arthur Rimbaud, Nikola Vaptsarov.

GOOD SCIENCE

GOOD SCIENCE

The drill sergeants break up the only road we've got
The angry woman rings it starts to rain
I state my case on the basis of need
You shoot it down on the basis of want

This week has given me a new grasp of particle physics
You see how the glands in your throat do swell
So profitability extends to the Silurian layers
The Dow is up the unit starts to break down

A light plane trails red fly north-west orient
I've managed to lie down on the floor just once
The embarrassment factor peaked now & again
Neoclassicism was a reaction to this "dangerous future"

My legs started to shake uncontrollably
They are not objects but networks of relationships
She was smoking & talking for the first time
A threequarter century rhythm punctuates diurnal priorities

Morosely a pearly king & queen get off the train
A gunshot spoils the tidal rhythm
Take away the underlying phrase-length & improvisation remains
Does fortune play the strumpet with me now?

It was a projection outward of active perception
It was my muscles starting to open up
Maybe get sunflowers for the sunny wall
Her voice is a beautiful city that doesn't exist

We spent a most pleasant evening thank you
Liberated from the bar-line the grid-lit slabs reverberate
I tend to dissolve into the usual
You couldn't take more than an hour so left

After a heavy day the book was no more than adequately clear
The pound started trembly the board sent the dollar down
Now there's no objective way of measuring space
So the room moves into & out of phase with my conception

The elephant house is blinded with plywood
It contains the ghosts that language doesn't need
I could have gone to the music but didn't feel like it
You could have had salt beef rice & mixed pickle

Small children lay multicoloured hoops on the new tarmac
Contrast the yellow-grey gloom & the white glare
Extended intervals are occurring
It pervades my whole life at the moment

I bought a book on the subject & immediately felt guilty
They stayed in bed arbitrarily distanced
The big building is full of really crazy people
The man is 22 & has 2 tattoos

She cites brachiation as the original divergence
Scored for 6 bass clarinets & 6 contrabass clarinets
You dovetail neatly into the above stuff
I wake up I open the refrigerator I don't know where I am

A WALK BY THE VANISHED POWDERMILL

a sonata for w.m.

1

Which begins: an early morning
in a high European capital.
The band marches past half-
disassembled scaffolding
hits orange vertigo somewhere
between the majestic sweep
of the Andes & bad plumbing.

      Trombones &
      notes in shallow baskets
      & much later about 12 poets
      drunk below a viaduct —

Into this mess swoops a siren a monument
a savings bank the moment
déménagement slips your lips a stranded
tourist crocodile gapes the gap extends
to half tended gardens scooped
a disappeared gunpowder magazine
overlooking the confluence.
This powerful wall is almost breathtaking
we go to the very nice "Pétrusse" park
down freedom street
we enjoy viewing the viaduct
a redoubtable redoubt is manifest here.

      Also the museum is closed
      fermé, fermato, cerrado.

2

A three-way babble
in variegated light
white blue red
that's OK so street level
you can see anything
that way never begin
again never return lost light
pressure at the base of the neck
in flooded colour
dream or drift down a sky slope
lose the city

continually

dissolve or drown in your body
hold your voice

the book slips from your hand this
fragile admission's very lovely/terrifying
mingled with perfume & heavy
shivery changeable day.
Oh wake up for heaven's sake
kick out the loops.
There are certain crucial elements missing
in this room but love is in it.

3

Where has the powdermill disappeared to?
It's not there on the magnificent hilltop.

Nor down below in the mysterious valley
where you're not supposed to go.

Regard the bridge. It weighs thus many
metric tonnes I forget. There are 119

others plus of course the viaduct which presides
over our ramshackle funny lives.

4

I'm sitting in the civic square now waiting
for you to come by. On the stand
the band plays A Life on the Ocean Wave
the burgers strut the tables are jolly
red & white the cloths nipped to them by
steel calipers. Your absence is manifest everywhere.
Long cables hold the trees together
they are like cables of love
but here is an interruption.

One of those where you don't can't
get it all but it makes your brain
stand on end with its implications how
long can this go on? We have the rest
of our lives for such grand passion & lack
of co-ordination and it didn't matter
then energy flooded back:
do you have the picture? with the paper
held up front? what pattern will emerge?

> As it happens this wonderful
> flavour explodes in your mouth
> like *il pubblico della poesia*
> applauding without as one or
> tossing sawdusty bread rolls
> into this hotel room perchance
> which is a kind of non-euclidean
> space which is sweet —

Cross it out.

Put sugar in your coffee.
Kick up the blanket. Utterly
change your life.

BLAZE

for Joseph Beuys

Semen and
menstrual blood
stain the shelf
surround

an inventor
of metaphors
an idiot
refuses

wholly
a tool without
blood on it
means naked

people with
animals took
him out of this
crash heap

so he
related such
material to
the social body

to a screen
image to a
broken line
suddenly

crumbled it
looked
secure but
blood reaches

to the throat
the terror
region
a drum rally

into a steeple
geese fly
the basic
stuff of risk

luminous
through the
webbed skeleton
or through

assembled dirt
for contemplation
a small book
during the war

immediately
possible for
human discipline
meaning

more basic
to warmth
more basic to
coldness

collapse began
to damage
the rule
structure

to come
to that again
wailing through
the long

work
in wood stain
his courage
phases

in fields
far from holy
flocks or
trails

coarse gritty
abandoned
moist poignant
a kind of

real other
excavation
of nail-paring
shadow

lasts for
1,000 years
then vacates
the building

physical flesh
to become
windstream
a new sculpture

a wound that
doesn't
know its own
price

a gauge
of what is
likely
to take place

a crown that's
melted to an
animal born
gold

mixed with
alcohol
transformed
to peace

or a tree
with a
stone is
beautiful

LASHED TO THE MAST

1

The timer clicks
     the flame bursts
        the children
were found wandering in the
    garden
— afraid
       to spin madly
   into this white book —
      "the walls just fell away"
 "I had expected
    serious injuries even
  some fatalities so I was
    pleasantly surprised"
watch the nets a
   crisis in the nasal passages
    they will decide
  whether to
     testify
       you know that
heaven &
   earth was
lashed
    "I did not paint it
    to be enjoyed"

*

Blood
   enters the painting & a
   weary languor fills my wallet

while up
            stairs the sirocco burns
            the leaves off the pods off

oh my
            when will the summers of old
            return to transfigure the future

being
            a representation of what you can
            never have like California sex

so that
            we shall meet again in the fields but
            shan't remember our names or why

and call
            mother mother it's no use the water's
            burning the wind the water the sun

            *

One evening the sky looks
like a Rothko heavy pink-grey
bearing down on a band of ice-blue
the next it's a mottled burst
spread from its milky heart behind
the offices it is driving you quite mental
& even hopeful but strange
lumpish cloud returns today
to hide the rest of the universe

            *

19

Worries about Money
      make chemical changes
            in the mind which are boring
in the blood
            stains fade into the post-
modern pattern
            of the bed
      which could be runic
all the sixes
            clickety click
      the station
            meets the train
                  with a shy
smile
      halfway
                  goddess in high
      heels
                  (white) (representing
Money)
            welcomes travellers to our
                  Heritage
                        economic growth &
prospects of artistic wonder
      pointed the phone at the Moon
            said we'll shoot it down
                  a planet hovers
perilously

*

It is a terrible thing
to be walking on a string
and never
to fall

20

I did this all night long
and I was not wrong
to wake

it was not morning nor bloody

my new home
's roof is patched
its downpipes coming away
but I wake
in it

it is in my veins & heart
beating & making a weak
form like a sentence implied
by its punctuation

or like four walls imply
a space

*

Oh
    such
        wonderful
    style
                posing
        all over
                the
        super-
    structure
        in your
designer
    jeans
        & being

21

consumed
   with the
         in-
effable —
   bought of
         ponderables —
though all thought
   fled
       from your head
six shamans
   or men or she-men
   invade your dream
         my bloody Valentine

*

At the end
all that will
be left is
the depth of
sunlight fall-
ing on the
ancient trucks
way beyond
your capacity
to comprehend
and the sense
of a name
that constantly
eludes your lips
and leads you
into delusion
that language
is merely
a question
of naming

2

Two people speak &
a third observes
from afar
their body gestures their eyebrows
& from this
draws a conclusion

A fourth says the
terrible words

And a fifth & sixth —

Can they tell you a secret
he was in Mexico with a friend
the building buckles
into the gulf which
forms in the interstices
of our syntax

And a train roars past
carrying the seventh

to the point of no return

*

As a star turns blue
in gathering crépuscule

you become that small pleasure

just drop your shoulders
and the word skips out

it's only a word

But a word is worth
a thousand pictures

I thought I saw a kestrel
fly over the high street

moving its darkness swiftly
below the pearly light

the clouds made

*

I do not spurn
        the hand of friendship
                and yet
    there is so little
        that I can say

                when the red jewels
        pass into the night
I am so hot
    I shiver with it
hands on the bricks

        there was a road
            we began

    and it is not ended

sometimes there are fire-
                            works
        beyond the gilded
                    buildings

I think of you then
        & all the selves
                you could have been

        *

    Strange
            thought: to
continue
            undecidably so
        for
            where events
        have seemed to
            crash
                    &
                            billow
        they have fallen
            kindly
                    in the end

        & it is no part
            of face
                    value
    to deny them
            their momentum
        of speculative
            grace

        *

There was never enough wine
            poetry's line has been cut
a berk lays claim to its energy

25

                yet kinship is fostered even
across the ocean of dreams
                in a celebrated scrawl
sweet burned chicken
                secure against wind & money
fills three ravening stomachs
                she mends her broken house
while he prepares to leave his
                & both part from the third
where the foundations rise
                & plane trees lie akin
to a slew of happiness

*

A
    quite
        appalling
                            hamburger
                marks
    our parting
                anew
    (whoever
                someone
thought we were)
                across
    the ocean
                of foolishness
    a raft
        we
                have
                        named
        wisdom

3

Quilted by what sea
          my blunt fingers
snuggle up
          to a world of wonders
customs/pigeons/
          Bantu warriors/laundrette/
abandoned supermarket
          salty through the throat
headlights flicker
          on the dark bodies
in the theatre
          with no name

*

(from the Spanish)

As soon as I fall asleep
there are the spaces
where my face becomes snow
high, in the territory

And when I embark
with my heart in shadow
I take this writing with me
below the level of consequence

And each night is a new
infancy, of a profile
sufficient to destroy
the language of my rusty years

*

(for Olivier Messiaen)

A Paradise of
Birds
Tropicals the
Night

When the music
Stops
It is as though
Nothing
Begins

*

Just a bright desk-lamp
     & the warm
     cuddle of the
     air between
these 4 walls takes you through
     to the mid-
     point of the day
     when you repair
to the Star across the road
     for sustenance
     in a foggy
     dream of a
space between the fragilities

*

Dig into
the
depths a

      wish
      wells
      up

      (is it
choreography or is it
         dance?)

      it's on the
      cards
      it's in the
      stars

blind we
bat
a lid
in the
black
night

      a
      brilliance
      beyond

*

Sluttish prevarication &
dreadful sloth
creep upon me in the sadness
of winter
      my friend of strange
foggy furloughs

My sunny days
are spangled upon the folds
of memory flashing up
in fits I love to behold
it is at such times I'd saddle
a recalcitrant mule & take to the lemon
groves that braid some mountain

where the Catholic monarchs
confront the Moorish dynasties
across a word-processed valley
or across the orbit of a TV satellite
in the dying of the sun

But the white noise
of a no-signal screen remains —
were I to reach to switch
that off
I'd switch the darkness on

DEEP SONG

GRANADA/EL CHORRO/RONDA, 1987

May a small thing become large
& make of such worry a tired fabric
that seems delicate? In the kitchen,
white food. Smoke fades
linearly. Dogs peter into the distance
a roule of disturbance in the night's suburb
in the night's night, covering half
a still discovered globe. The roofs
bunch. What cannot be said is
how deep it goes, into the lissom dark,
a plaint, or a cycle of intention—
a left hanky on a golden lit table
a couple of books offering content
its substitute, the small medicine
anticipating its disease. But those hills
wasting into mist, where are they?
the lace upon them & the colour
blue? Before them stand the buildings of a kingdom
half integrated with the wood
& offering the dead sun its reflectance
a facade & colonnade for the entry
of the weapons of nostalgia that
stupid cry of the heart
representing trophies, though
presently far & immune
from such shapely rhetoric wanting
out of love's habit to hold a life & sensing
uncertainty. Colour fails through
three inclined trapezoidal panels
& stars of eight & sixteen points
decorate the whole composition. A lovely
geometric surrounds its most solemn acts
& beyond, the towers become water
& just fade away. Water does

converge. And that makes a cue
an infinitely reversible sign
for return to night, the city, all that this
means. That is to say this
species of absence out of which
& towards which every page spirals
so making of presence & absence
the coordinates. And in the cunningly
divided room with rectangular areas in shadow
you will also believe this. Or better,
you will abandon belief & cover
the fretted self arrayed
with text & fragrant hibiscus
flowers in another night, in a night
that is not this already slipping from you.

A Generating Station in Andalucia

Green — I want you —
Not the mysterious reservoir —
            Nor its appearance in a hot valley
        As a still element, perhaps of grief — no —
            Green of the north
How novel it looks
        on the ground & on the trees

I want to wake up
            In my new home — in the city
Green, rhythmic
            traffic of it steals sleep
From the gathering autumn

Breathe deep & simultaneously
            The stars hide their turbulence
Behind a pall that inserts
        Above the still dark air a thought

            Is the self of thought
            the same as the self
            that writes the thought?
            the command centre at the
            heart of a mountain?
                            Is it
            the difference between
            ritual & habit? The dark
            hills wait. The sky
            is black. Where

35

did a thought come
from? & what faint
sound from the lit bars
at night will take me
back there?

The shining flat
water reflects four
terrible floodlights
among derricks &
piers. Beyond the dark
hills are the black
mountains & beyond,
the unimagined sky. Four
lights hum in night's
fragrance. The Pleiades
above the mountain
blur.

And now that green is flecked
    It whites up on you
  What do I care
    as you dive into the pool

The water is not separate
  From the body, and the body
    As it moves through the water
  Is not wet

Only as you move into the sun does the water cling
    And become separate

Far below, and scarcely
perceived — lemon
or olive groves braided
across a mountain, scarcely
do snake track, light
pools, dust shading
to deep green in bluish
air, cling to the surfaces.

You go up that mountain & immediately
    you go to sleep
        It washes your mind
    Out from the inside —
        You are discovered by a gypsy —

You sit outside on the terrace typing
    And the mountains — more blue now —
        & their braids —
    I was talking to you about my friend:
We were on a high road amid white
        flowers & eucalyptus, it was only
    when I woke I knew

    But it was real, or it partook of something
You wouldn't even call real, you're
        in it, actually

You go to sleep, & it washes
    your mind out —
I go to the mountain & there is a little tank
    Of still green water I look into —
        It's hot, & the silence
    Bounces thus off the hills around
I take a photograph of the mountain

        Up the valley advanced
        Tariq's army covered by
        earth. Now bones, store-
        houses, entry places
        & wells appear. A
        thousand years arch
        out of the rock, a cock
        crow greets short
        rain spotting the tiles
        in grey. The sun begins
        to push its whiteness
        through, but cover slips
        up from the horizon.

    Look at me
        I don't know you now
You move through the water
        Afraid to touch its limitless
    limits —

We were both sitting on the edge
    Of the stagnant water tank he said
"So long" & dropped
    It was some years before he hit the water —

Your keys & espadrilles
Laid neatly on a stone beside you

Half a porcelain cup
on the terrace's round
table's circled by a fly.
The breeze begins.

I found you lying
as though asleep
on the side of a
mountain, as though
you'd got off the train
of thought & failed
to get back on.

Look at me, he said — the water
Sparkling in the sun because it moves

You sit on the terrace in your dark
Glasses & your headscarf in the photograph
That was before —

Old buzzing
fly languidly
persists, nearby —
heaves blackish
body in erratic
motion from
corner to corner
of the almost
darkened room —

And now the thought has gone, and
        only its words remain —
    Their demands blur
        into the wash
Green.
        I want —

RILKE DRIVING SCHOOL

Composing a latter-
Day *ghazal* here
Am I leaning
On the corner
Of the *Calle
Carlos Marx*, a
Taste as of
Lemon in my
Mouth, a real
Nexus of energy!
While Rilke,
Now transformed, a
Metal man
Stands in the
Garden of the
Hotel Queen
Victoria, Ronda,
Gazes into a
Future that
Hangs perilously
Limpid over the
Chasm, a fever
That becomes
Almost palpable. What
Substance wavers
And weaves? Who
Do you cling
To when it
Happens? when the
World opens up
Under your feet,
When its substance
Vanishes, what is
Your resource when

No meaning
Happens, when
Stuff is rent?
And why
Do I recall
This on the
Train much
Later, gold giving
Way to silver
In the cloud
Streaks that
Halo industrial
Estates & playing
Fields of south
London? But I
See it's the
Wrong train, the
Network must be
Negotiated anew.
I love you
Very much, even
After you reach
A certain point
On your progress
Down the hill,
When the sun
Disappears behind
Some crystals &
Suddenly you are
In shadow. Not
Too dismal, chucking
Out tons of
Rubbish, I'm re-
Born, almost.
Perhaps momentous
Changes have left
Me physically.

*

Rilke: I am
Older & sometimes
Physically horizontal.
Here is the
Photo, little
Poet with his
Hand resting on
Big poet. Hmm.
His bag &
Camera thus.
Oh to be
Metal, to no
Longer crumble
Fast from the
Pressure but to
Rust slowly
Under a deep
Blue Spanish sky,
To be metal
And glass. Why
Cling? It's no
Use when momentous
Changes impend.
For example, this
Evening a car
Whisks me off
To a surreal
Interview, I just
Had to sit
Back in the
Sticky leatherette.
I love you,
I was seized
With a desperate
Fear I dared

Not convey,
Trembling in the
Bedroom much later.
Roots crack, seeds
Germinate, two
Locomotives fall in
Love down a
Suburban chasm. The
Fear has dissipated
Like foam
Upon the water.
You approach me:
Temperatures do
Now fluctuate.

*

Yesterday I was
All arms &
Thumbs, nervously
Circling the flat.
And a wintry
Light all week.
Today I am
Walking on air,
I am almost
Above the brink
Of the gorge
In that garden
With Rilke to
Blot my idiot
Remarks into
Its waters. We
Walk calmly,
Discussing, it is
Almost as though

We're in the
World. *Cut.*
Put on my
Scarf & walk
Into the winter-
Less winter
Whose first few
Moments baffle my
Brain, playing Muslim
Blues; a demon
Closed my eyes
In the garden
Of the Queen
Victoria, your right
Thigh against me.
But you were
Never there; I
Love you, it's
An emergency.
Buildings shudder
To their deaths
But your grip
Is firm. Someone
Is breathing
Slowly on the
Train while a
Walkman idly
Spits. The train
Comes to a
Shuddering halt,
Awakes me from
Dream. Hesitation.
Glad of these
Contours, my hands
Change colour in
Celebration of you.
Sunshine is

In the picture
To which we
Shall certainly
Return. A poem
Is like a
Story, except liquid
With echo. White
Letters far below
Indicate the unassailable
Distance to square
Fields, the colours
Oily the timber
Stacked the estate
Real the plunder
Partly the water
Flat with reedy
Clog & animal
Magic, lemons
Left to rot
In the warm
Heart of the
Old country. A
Poem is like
A story except
Nobody knows
What it means.
Woke up before
It was light,
Eager to
Let the day
Begin. In my
Fitful dream
There was even
More happy
Confusion. I go
Up that mountain
And return, legs

Trembling, speaking
Nonsense through an
Empty tube that
Boggles the
Archives, the shadow
Moving on the
Wall, the landscapes
Beneath us, &
Roads of especial
Touristic interest, ie
Terrifying. Dance
Of light in
Water. The glitter-
Ing fragments
Wept. It was
Because I never
Thought there was
Anyone who
Could tell me
What they
Were. You are
Magnified a million
Times. Water moves
In your eyes
Briefly. White
Light on tennis
Courts, on bowling
Green, the ropes
Of steel.

BAD SIRENS

AFTER A SEASON THE SYNTAX FALLS

for Doug Oliver

Through your half-window
    a little blues must fall
    on midnight's alien heart
    morale fragments

And you don't want the visit
    to end, the terrible new
    that hugger-mugger steals the echo
    while knowing its origin fled

But it wasn't choice, & weakness
    fills your body, giving
    it colour & stain & every
    rhetoric of the interval

The evening was white at first but
    blackening to ripeness
    the language stayed on hold
    the roofs portended

A perfume of turbid
    rain, a great plain oak
    laid on its side among bracelets
    among the streets

A rusty tip, a wisp of blue
    solicited your viral ecstasies
    entered the audit like a ghost
    a white band of dust around your brains

When from no time a bad siren screamed
    into the night — the white
    narcissus must grow loaded now
    your hand on the cup dishevels

You wake into a swoon
    a barium meal lights up your heart
     in the temperate city
    you will never see again

You're in the street: a crowd
    outside the surgical building
    waits to be threaded, three
    by three up the crooked wood

To a fortress, a dark fact
    a horseshoe steeply raked
    above the bare brilliance where it's
    crammed, condemned to watch

Where young attendants
    come & go, chalk scribbles
    on the conference board, then more
    till the composition obscures

They feed white noise in
    to make believe it's quiet
    a woman says: "It's a small world
    either that or a big hospital"

What is this place? a surplus value
    of meaning? the way a shadow
    falls, drains into poetry, the way
    a shadow falls the way a shadow falls

An elephant bears a turret, frankly
    naff, a flare illuminates the place
    of silence, engine blanketed
    cloud-cover building grid

A bank of 20 screens
    & a glaze of money on each one
    you feel that it all must have
    happened a long time ago

The numbers rise & fall
    implacably serene you place
    a child's compass next the cathode ray
    its needle spins round madly

How briefly this machine
    flickers under glass & then
    is still — sleeves your flesh
    into the vinyl

What was a factory or church
    becomes a theme park
    what was a hospital becomes
    a hologram of commerce

Its first replica, your father
    trembles on the bed
    your mother has no verbs
    for her mistake

Places the logical value "false"
    within a cell, the heart
    which generates an error
    a principle of depth

It's unredeemable, a botch
    turns mental sex into a monster
    to be done in comprehensively
    in the place of silence

Where the residual heat is found
    to crack walls, no ventilation
    no light, an inside job
    classed as a family

Where a man with a spike
    hacks at a piece of composite
    a venerable shibboleth
    an assessment of trauma

Where a sad pale one approaches
    on the uneven platform
    as a voice begins again to chide
    endlessly: Mind the gap

Who extends a supplicant hand
    needing to go to a coastal town
    needing for this six pounds
    you give him one

Or at another station one approaches
    matching sadness with belief
    needing to go to the Horn of Africa
    needing your answer to his question

On the actual train, a lovely
    couple: he holds a giant tin
    of coffee, rusting all the while
    she cuddles a restless guinea-pig

Another leans against a jamb
    he cannot move he can
    not move, save to launch a sluggish
    Indian meal on the wine-dark tarmac

All go to the enterprise meltdown
    though the glass be smashed
    and the wafer skin grey
    that held Communitas

Serrated, almost noble once
    though the very veins broke
    in a welter of logic bombs
    where the oaks do lie

There are no maps here but
    a hoarding sells you worms
    with designer-brain finance
    the public flock to null

Thwarted by thrones
    so evidently respectful
    not anchored in sufficiency
    but tethered in want

Fitting to be savaged
    & thrust into a neuro-surge
    which is really a market that
    masquerades as body scan

Like a pricing-gun, tension
    speaks, stops, stutters
    the heat abates & turns to thin rain
    outside the place of silence

You stumble to the street —
    in its broken booth a phone rings
    endlessly all-night TV reflected in a window
    victims & supermarket trolleys

A woman ghost — "I've been here 20 years
        waiting for a 188" — & socialism's born
        & dies, while unctuously a distant radio
        grieves your mouth explodes

In a vast pool of undrained mud
        parked hatchbacks left, first sound
        of birdsong, a rusty tip a wisp
        of blue, & mad poetry fills your sense

All this you see through
        your high lustre window
        or is it your punch blushed
        face that rebounds?

Are they the same old bones that
        rattle in the same old tin?
        does half of the imagery
        curve into the same error?

You are there in heat the
        colour closing down
        down 40, rose falling
        glad of a transient

Through your half-window
        a little blues must fall
        a scent of history trembling
        at the wrists of never

LEXICAL DUB

"Secret secret never seen
secret secret ever green"
– popular song

Police glossolalia haunt radio heavy wind
Instruments of use in time of war
From here to Texas burgeoning

An offence an offence (as officially defined)

We wage war on all the animals that come to live with us

An offence such an offence

Teams finger the ethics of punishment
A gunboat to Morocco had become an epidemic   The Agadir
                                                             crisis, 1911
On blood red screen man washes car with hosepipe
That person shall be guilty of a misdemeanour
Approaches or is in the neighbourhood of or enters
Each occupied square is surrounded by 8 squares

Any prohibited place possession or control

Looks like colour xerox & feels like a total effect

Any sketch plan model article note document
Or information like when real blood appears
On video screen music
Swells to gothic cancerous zombies superimpose
If any person communicates or retains he
Shall be liable to imprisonment with or without
Hard labour
Any work of defence arsenal factory
Dockyard camp ship telegraph or signal station or office

Any ship arms or other materials or instruments
Of use in time of war or any plans or documents
Demand paralysis respect for rule of law
Any railway road way or channel
Declared by a Secretary of State to be a prohibited place
Shall be a prohibited place

*

Edition of
*The London
Programme*
on heroin
addiction,
transmitted
13.iv.84,
London
Weekend TV
Starts with £5 scag bags on the council estates
Or any place used for gas water or electricity works
Ends with novocaine mainlined into tongues
To protect official secrets & get us out
Of a bad situation *vis-à-vis* that which endures
Or any place where any ship arms or other materials
Or instruments of use in time of war

*

Speech by
Lord Haldane,
1911; see
article by
Peter Kellner
in *New
Statesman*,
6.iv.84
Not many months ago we found in the middle of the
Fortifications at Dover an intelligent stranger
Who explained his presence by saying
He was there to hear the singing of the birds
Any offence an offence the offence the offence
Incites or counsels or attempts to procure

An offence an offence an offence that offence

Official
Secrets Act,
enacted
22.viii.11,
after going
through all
stages in the
Commons in
less than an
hour
Two men got up to speak but both were forcibly pulled down
By their neighbours after they had uttered

Such an offence an offence such an offence

A few sentences again they were pulled down
By their neighbours the vote 107–10 (500 abstentions)
One hot Friday afternoon in August
If a justice of the peace is satisfied

58

Things went a bit far he may grant a search warrant
Authorising any constable to seize
If necessary by force and to search and to search
Any sketch plan model article note or document
All acts which are offences when committed or when committed
Having been or being about to be committed

*

In 1981 crucial
Molotov cocktails make white goods blush
Crunched underfoot in a skin of acid rain
From here to Texas looks like colour xerox
No hope no future
Cancel future with instant response
Police cruise total exclusion zone
Pre-emptive in the service
In 1984 an example must be made
An offence the offence an offence
Include any communicating or receiving
Include the copying or causing to be copied
Between an unquestioned & unquestionable Secret Vote
Include the transfer or transmission
Punishable under this Act this Act may be cited
In defence of instruments of use in time of war

Document includes part of a document

Numbers of union leaders start to disappear

Model includes design pattern and specimen

Peruvian flutes indicate primitive lisping apparatchiks

Sketch includes any photograph or other mode of representing

Dogs give voice in the echoing car-park

Riots in Brixton, Toxteth and elsewhere, summer 1981

cf. Sex Pistols, c.1977

Sentence of 6 months on Sarah Tisdall for disclosing information to *The Guardian* on the arrival of Cruise missiles

Offence under this Act includes
Any act omission or other thing
Which is punishable under this Act

*

See: Duncan
Campbell,
*Big Brother
is Listening*
(1981) Fish stains guttering peach police glossolalia
Identify any person
Other than a person acting under lawful authority
Daddy's dead riot squad riot
Notwithstanding that no such act is proved against him
He shall be guilty of felony
Any constable must have a plan for copious stinking water
It shall not be necessary to show that the accused person
Was guilty of any particular act
He may be convicted
Before everything disappears everything disappears
Xerox handcoloured by dayglo marker
Political conviction not allowed

A person that person any person
Other than a person acting under lawful authority

In lunar months weeks playing cards alphabet

The offence an offence
An offence an offence
An offence such an offence
An offence an offence an offence that offence
Such an offence an offence such an offence
An offence an offence are offences

If necessary by force

Such an offence

60

INCIDENT ROOM

Might have been carnival
Perpetual beauty flanked by soft sculpture horses
Glowing orange on one side
And ashen silver on the other
But it all segues into transmitter information
Unstable in the day's winds

And the underlying belief
On the streets
That those humans are not human
And the same again   is made manifest
        Rain soaked
Floodlit prison to one side
Vast hospital ventilation to the other
Inner city where
To have your feet on the ground is both privilege
And punishment
The serial & consecutive reality of it

On the one hand choice
On the other no choice at all
When love turns to violence
To have to say it the insistence
The first & worst word
That breaks the spell
Just kills you

AND 'MID THIS TUMULT

You can't get away from it. Take
For instance the french golden delicious
Increasingly perishing in their chinese baskets
Hung above the table. A helicopter now hangs in the middle
Of the air I breathe, only further away —
And even further, 2 jet trails in the evening sky, & further
Than that still the american space shuttle
In its phallic transformation mounts
Away solidly from Cape Canaveral
Which isn't Kennedy any more why not
So you get a sense that it all makes sense
Which in present circumstances political & economic
Can only surface as paranoia.
For instance sometimes you get too much
Information about a thing & then
That information is withdrawn.
The helicopter's rotors cleverly slice
Several of the apples in half —
That's technology for you
Nothing is safe any more it's amazing.

A New Word Order

When all is said & done, then
There is everything still to say & do;
As when, growing much older, one starts to become
Less interested in meanings, more in the look, the sound. Under
Our very feet the stars clump: Procyon, Rigel,
Aldebaran. Or do they? Is it just possible they are no more
Than linguistic sequences, a banal melody that
Merely happens, like, preset 200,000 times
Precisely, regardless of need? We switch
200,000 times between event & grid. *Cut.* A European city at night
Is spread before us: on the late bus
The ensemble sings a raucous song, draws smiley eyes on the wet glass
Before leaving on an endless quest for the classless society. Within
The incipient rain-forest in an under-construction bank foyer
The juicy realistic look of nature takes shape; the phone network
Evolves an ecology of its own, but crashing all the time; in the hotel
The security ring wanders round in white stockings & panties
Developing the right attitude to eroticism; in a building
The size of a small airport 107 delegates
Are trying to liberalise world trade. *Cut.*
The words of the press release, once incandescent, fly
Into the spaces the edge left. (There's no edge.)
Fire, blood & alphabet, as Lorca says,
But now lacking ardour, haemoglobin: it's a game
Where facetiousness
And seriousness are inseparable; where
The jocular and the intimate form a badinage
Which conceals, reveals for a moment,
Then conceals again. On the other hand
Things are more like they are now
Than they ever were before.
Things is things, and words is words; the game *is* a game,
A free lunch *is* a free lunch,
It is no longer a metaphor, a penis *is* a penis, a cigar

Is a cigar,

A razor that senses the individual needs of your face

Is a razor that senses the individual needs of your face.

And it somewhat follows that two-dimensional thrust-vectoring
exhaust nozzles with cold-start droop and gun turrets slaved to
helmet sights, combined with fire-&-forget carbon-fibre
reinforced integral throat entrance structures *are* what they
seem, a superabundance of gas, food, beauty & drugs. Whatever
it takes.

Cut.

A vain attempt lurks on the cusp. The cusp of what?

Badinage is when you're bad but really it's good.

*

Dark rain. Begin again.

Dark shadows everywhere, yellow light seeps, but above

There's a paler sky, getting ready to precipitate.

More horizon than fact, sheet steel becomes water on the reservoir,
clotted with seabirds, and rooks hunched on posts on the
sandbags, yet

It's a desert, that is, a place of language,

Or you could say:

The canopy of the firmament, held aloft by the ancient god, but that

Doesn't work any more.

In Washington today the White House spokesman said: "It's not
necessary

To create beauty but, hell, let's do it anyway." Forty-two per cent

Of the American people back the President, forty-eight per cent are
against,

Ten per cent don't know. In London

The FT 100 simpers & blushes, a rush of gold to the head,

Of oil & gold, the pound

Peeps shyly out from its basket

Of currencies, the metaphoric unreality

Of such events no longer cuts against

Their cinematic truth. It is good, & fashionable too

For walls to tumble — one nation, one people,
Many cell-phones — such simple rules, such
Complicated behaviour!
On the minus 4th day of Xmas,
His running shoes dedicated to the goddess Nike,
A less than magnificent jogger stumbles by
Plunging into & out of tunnels of mathematics
Humming the ballad of Peckham Rye
Beneath the enormous sky; is interfered with by an expostulant
    jaywalker
Shrouded in glory, babbling of
Jesus in a strange hat. *Cut* to interior, close-up,
As if the telescopic view had of a sudden become microscopic:
A gecko marvellously switches
Between action & inaction, an incredible device
With suckers on his feet, for the distempered wall;
Caked with mould,
A tiny tonal jewel, a chemical flambeau — not much else on the box
    these days you notice — montages onto the
Golden thigh of a handsome woman to intelligently
Erotic effect, it being beyond the 9pm watershed, but 'tis pity
She can't act, looks like
Her DNA built out of plywood 'stead of protoplasm.
There are chemicals in the solid media air, chemicals & heroes too,
    you can tell them by the inoffensive i.e. non-strobing suits they
    wear as they crawl up the wall, glistening, perfectly socialised
    — over to you, Francine — where was I? — in the protective
    maw of just another capitalist leviathan, benevolent is the word,
    & the word is the product, don't ever forget that, translated out
    of bodily fluids & not to be trusted. *Action!* The security grasps
    its corset suggestively. Various neighbours & their electronic
    devices make small noises in the night, figured as such & such
    rhetorical angels, moodily slumping or engaging in gay banter,
    it's much the same, squirrelling away their pathetic memories or
    (love *this* metaphor) disinterring them for a sniff, yuk, all save
    the one below who regularly burns his toast as a special daily
    offering to the tutelary god of forgetfulness, a parody of a

pastiche of a pariah if you ask me. Is there some wiggle room
here? I think not.
Listen.
Watch it.
Say the word.
Catch it.
I'm sorry. Can you take a message?
Don't mention it. Smoking or non smoking?
Send no money now. Say the word & I'll be there.
Oh happy day! The terrible thing will not now happen
Till tomorrow at least. Jumping out of the window, after all,
Isn't so dangerous — hitting the ground is.
But everybody hits the ceiling 'cause nobody can *get* to ground.
Meanwhile
Take care of the sound and the sense will take care of itself.
Nimble clouds sprint past in a gentler post-nuclear world whose
  voices sing diversely but combine polyphonically in the same
  apology & the same directive: I'm sorry there is no-one here to
  answer your call, but if you'd like to leave a message I'll get
  back to you.

*

Was there a time, then, when the word
And the action, word & thing
Coalesced, when the shape of it
Was not all that there was, & the other entirely
Over there? Was there, let's say, a ship
(Could you say ship, & would a ship then be here?)
Borne by the soft western breeze
Towards its destiny? And what was that destiny
If not a fusion of every possible script, once suspended
In a filigree trace of currents? Are we then plunged backward
Into the question of what happened, where blended
Into history's ancient faeces the father's corpse
Emerges, a real object transfigured
Close to the sacred?

66

Did the ship's crew & cargo, the foremothers
And forefathers, serenely poisoned baby-angels,
Assimilate the sunlight that silvered the water
Till the high cliffs broke upon their sight
And braids of sand-dunes, drainage patterns,
Ran out onto the gravel plain?

Did the ship cast down its anchor then,
Haloed with a paternal aura? Did the tribute children
Hum the descant in doubt & fear? And did they
Weep aloud because they were to become present, because
They should no more look on the earth?

Perhaps it was then the word split from its referent,
The woman from the child she had been, beginning to want to exist,
A sense of this intertwining, scatter-marking her arabesques,
Soft staining her density, reading its event
Into a single radiant symbol that stood
In relation to others & to the ground.

The man, then, would become defined by a hard pure line,
Tensed down into co-ordinates, into a horizontal and
Vertical role, not what is given
But the act of exchange itself.

Seized by desire to pour herself out, devastated,
The woman took these co-ordinates
Into her exploded body, & together they invented
Love & war. Love being to survive continuous
Cursive meaning, to become anyone at all, achieving senseless
Radiant death. And war? Well, suppose then the man
Twined his arm gently round her
And drew a heart, a penis, the sun,
Childlike marks against a light or dark ground,
Outlines in vivid geometry. And say the children, who now
Are no longer children,

Were brought each along the winding paths
To the labyrinth,
The most grand & fortified network of bunkers
Wherein hid a savage hybrid form for which no name
Existed. Then the world prepared for war.

Flame from the creature's mouth mingled with fat
Scorched the earth, & spread the devastation
From a field of diseased wheat in central Asia
To a battle tank in the Saudi desert. Here then is the word
And here the image, a whole system
Balanced upon a knife,
A string of numbers held on disk,
A contradiction held in check;
It is knowable, & it is normal. These, then,
These systems & sub-systems of representation,
Instruments of torture smeared or splashed
With frightful liquid, monsters against a copper ground
With frightful bodies or snouts peering
Across the far horizon: the copper-bottomed promises
Whose names are Lockheed, Aérospatiale,
McDonnell Douglas, Plessey; the shadow
On the land, the figure on the ground.

*

Action: figure on ground. In the depth
Of the city the homeless congregate; a
Restive silence lingers round the tight packed bodies
Covered in stab & other wounds, stained with petrol
And filigreed tattoos; they are children;
One says: "A work of art is not useless" but refuses
Elaboration; another: "The words are true, and the meanings are also
     true."
A third, squatting fatly between parked cars,
With hair dyed russet, screams at a black man "You're an animal!"
And, in mitigation:

"The way he's looking at me, his eyes are embarrassing me."
Here come the defence team, at this time, looking more than capable,
Hot as gods, with their Tango Charlie / Zulu Difference rap, the
    action of light
Reconciling them to their environment,
Their beautiful hands
Slapping the indifferent air, their genitals
Those of the spider, spinning a clue of thread, of
Soledad, or such demotic flair,
Their voices singing: "Hey, cunt, you left your face on my knee",
A thick miasma
Of acid rain & hashish steeping the trough, sweeping away
All residual ambiguity, i.e. *this* rather than *that*, a shadow of it,
    sweeping across the Western cities, to lie against the mountains
    which once were covered with forests of spruce, fir, pine &
    aspen to an elevation of 1,000 feet, their spectral signatures
    reflected off the earth at infrared wavelengths;
In their caves on the left hand side graffiti burnt into the fabric,
Marks of identity
Over the dancing waters, the happy days that will not return,
The virtuous circle that cannot be completed, the lack
That cannot be made good.

This has been made possible by our sponsors, the Sony corporation
And we would like to thank all those too numerous to mention.
Here they come, the Light Infantry, stepping so swiftly.

*

And then there was you. No, I hadn't forgotten.
You were sitting on the blue plastic seats in your black jacket, jeans
    and old trainers, warm, but interrupted by cloud.
You built a temple of money
Where a house of love should stand.

Who are you? a naked singularity
Trapped behind your personality's event horizon?

There isn't enough of you to tell, & yet I
Can't look at your eyes. You could be
What you've never known and can put no name to.
But, offered love, offered money & terror,
Your golden heart's secured by pins
To the set of a game show, its price named & named again.

Another time I saw you on the beach, but could not speak for
      personal reasons,
A third time reclining by the pool
At the house on the side of a mountain, looking down
On a fertile plain flowing with streams
From the field pattern
Of the world's oldest agriculture.

The lakes have disappeared;
Coded with the natural colours of the visible spectrum,
A local ecology of gardens now adorns
The homes of the privileged, salvaged from
The destroyed series. Lawns & golf courses
Lie further up the valley, resort beaches below;
The Strip runs north-south
And highways thread their way into the heat map
That has emerged. Car parks, warehouses, public buildings,
Piers & docks, and open pits & dumps
In saturated hues respond
To uses & abuses.

You're in the traffic with your companion, a song on the CD, a burst
      just peaking. The polarised glass, the crown. Like an analogue
      of the system itself. The lights change. Your head turns
      momentarily to the hidden sun's glint on a wide-bodied aircraft's
      wing, and you wonder where you saw that before. It is a crown
      of tremendously symmetrical main-sequence stars, made of
      words no-one can speak — we can say that it is like the world.
      But the world's grown old. It has become a habit.
The lights change.

Even though I invent the story of you, though I put in the detail, the
    answering machine, though I make it into a love story, as
    incandescent as a narrative without an ending can be, still your
    mouth says mutely that I have not yet reached you.
Make love, & put it right,
And if you can't make love
Make war, & put it right.
But never send to know for whom the lights change.

OTHER ROOF BOOKS

Andrews, Bruce. **Getting Ready To Have Been Frightened.** 116p. $7.50.

Andrews, Bruce. **R & B.** 32p. $2.50.

*Andrews, Bruce. **Wobbling.** 96p. $5.

Bee, Susan [Laufer]. **The Occurrence of Tune,** text by Charles Bernstein. 9 plates, 24p.$6.

Benson, Steve. **Blue Book.** Copub. with The Figures. 250p. $12.50

Bernstein, Charles. **Controlling Interests.** 88p. $6.

Bernstein, Charles. **Islets/Irritations.** 112 pp. $9.95.

Bernstein, Charles (editor). **The Politics of Poetic Form.** 246p. $12.95.

Brossard, Nicole. **Picture Theory.** 188p.$11.95.

Child, Abigail. **From Solids.** 30p. $3.

Davies, Alan. **Active 24 Hours.** 100p.$5.

Davies, Alan. **Signage.** 184p.$11.

Day, Jean. **A Young Recruit.** 58p. $6.

Dickenson, George-Therese. **Transducing.** 175p. $7.50.

Di Palma, Ray. **Raik.** 100p.$9.95.

*Dreyer, Lynne. **The White Museum.** 80p. $6.

Eigner, Larry. **Areas Lights Heights.** 182p. $12, $22 (cloth).

Gizzi, Michael. **Continental Harmonies.** 92p. $8.95.

Gottlieb, Michael. **Ninety-Six Tears.** 88p. $5.

Grenier, Robert. **A Day at the Beach.** 80p. $6.

Hills, Henry. **Making Money.** 72p. $7.50. VHS videotape $24.95.
    Book & tape $29.95.

Inman, P. **Red Shift.** 64p. $6.

Lazer, Hank. **Doublespace.** 192 p. $12.

Legend. Collaboration by Andrews, Bernstein, DiPalma, McCaffery, and Silliman.
    Copub. with L=A=N=G=U=A=G=E. 250p. $12.

Mac Low, Jackson. **Representative Works: 1938-1985.** 360p. $12.95, $18.95 (cloth).

Mac Low, Jackson. **Twenties.** 112p. $8.95.

McCaffery, Steve. **North of Intention.** 240p. $12.95.

Moriarty, Laura. **Rondeaux.** 107p. $8.

Neilson, Melanie. **Civil Noir.** 96 p. $8.95.

Pearson, Ted. **Planetary Gear.** 72 p. $8.95.

Perelman, Bob. **Face Value.** 72p. $6.

*Robinson, Kit. **Ice Cubes.** 96p. $6.

Seaton, Peter. **The Son Master.** 64p. $4.

*Sherry, James. **Part Songs.** 28p. $10.

Sherry, James. **Popular Fiction.** 84p. $6.

Silliman, Ron. **The Age of Huts.** 150p. $10.

Silliman, Ron. **The New Sentence.** 200p. $10.

Templeton, Fiona. **YOU-The City.** 150p. $11.95.

Ward, Diane. Facsimile (Photocopy of **On Duke Ellington's Birthday,**
    Trop-I- Dom, The Light American, and **Theory of Emotion**). 50p. $5.

*Ward, Diane. **Never Without One.** 72p. $5.

Ward, Diane. **Relation.** 64p. $7.50.

Watten, Barrett. **Progress.** 122p. $7.50.

Weiner, Hannah. **Little Books/Indians.** 92p. $4.

*Out of Print

For ordering or complete catalog write:
SEGUE DISTRIBUTING, 303 East 8th Street, New York, NY 10009